shapes

Photography
George Siede and Donna Preis

Louis Weber, C.E.O.
Publications International, Ltd.
7373 North Cicero Avenue
Lincolnwood, Illinois 60646

ISBN 0–7853–1283–8

Publications International, Ltd.

circle

flower

ball of yarn

buttons

bubbles

clock

square

blocks

present

checkerboard

washcloth

rectangle

wagon

letters

crackers

door

triangle

hat

musical triangle

flags

tent

heart

cake

locket

candy

valentine

oval

grapes

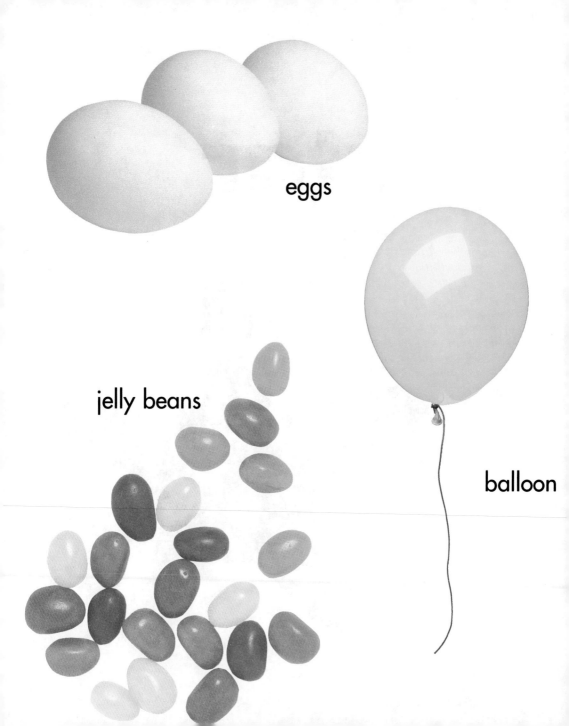

eggs

jelly beans

balloon

star

stickers

sea star

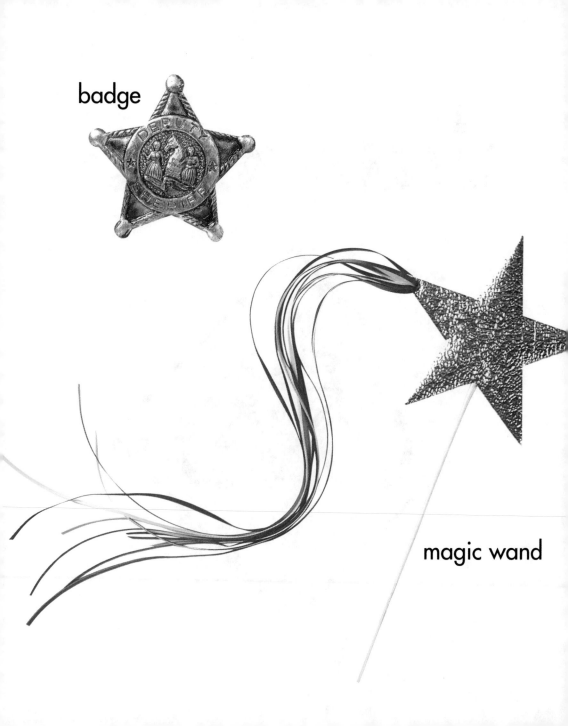

badge

magic wand

diamond

sign

cookie cutter

blocks

kite

shapes

circle

square

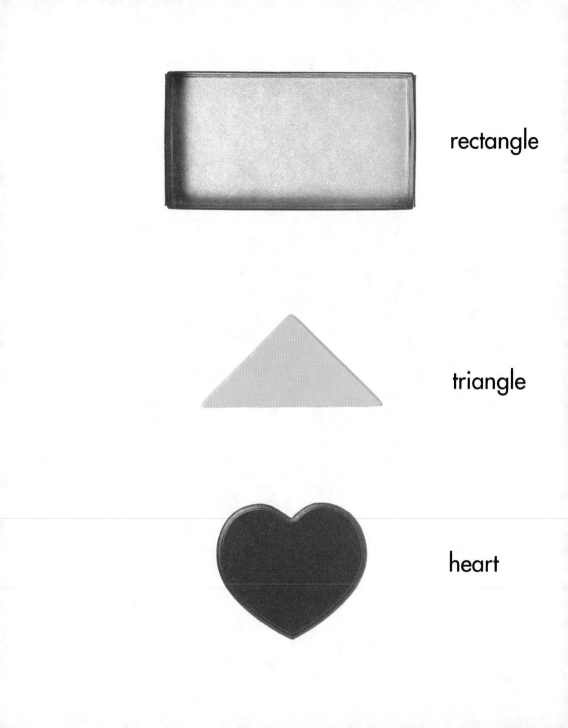

rectangle

triangle

heart